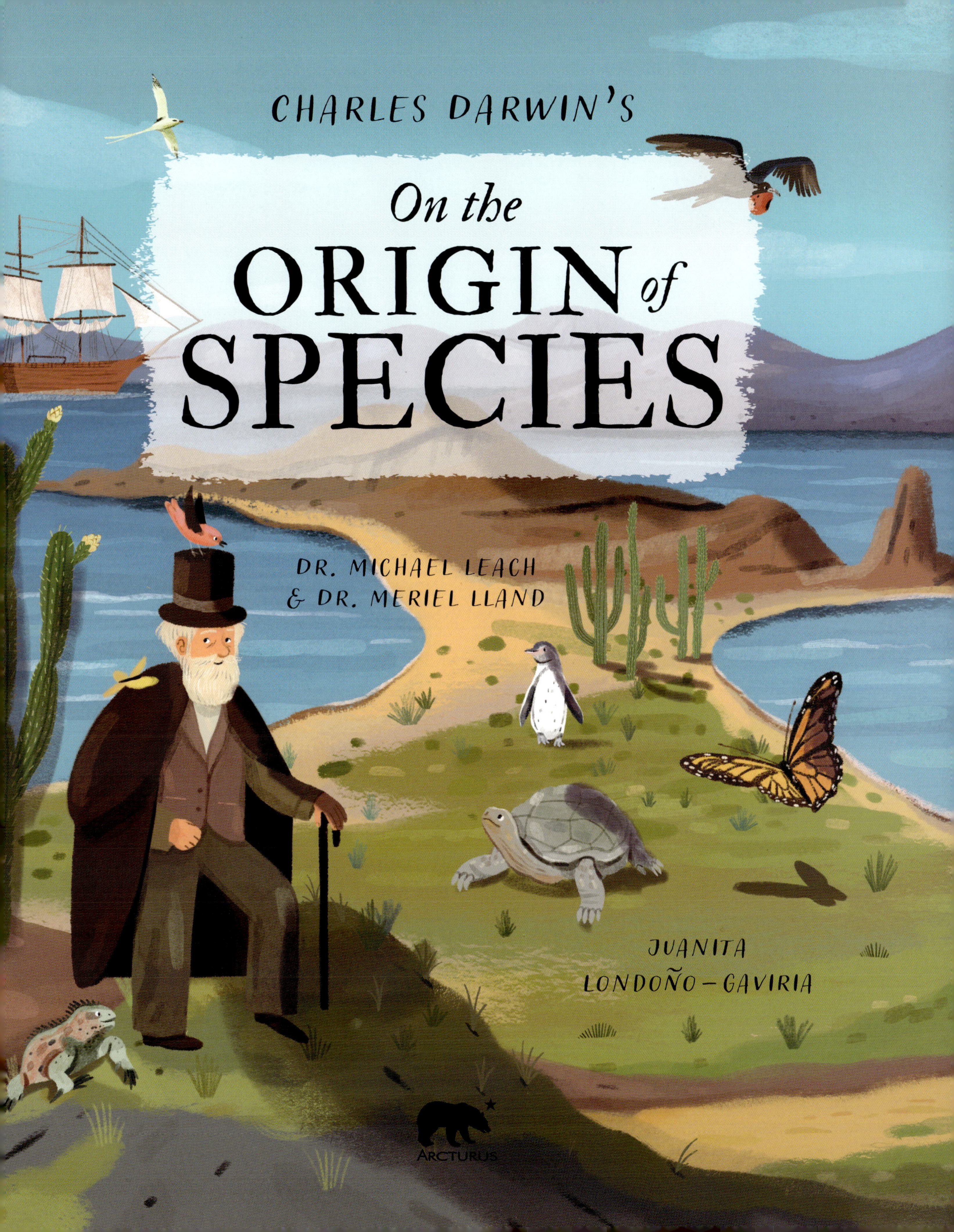
CHARLES DARWIN'S
On the
ORIGIN of
SPECIES
DR. MICHAEL LEACH
& DR. MERIEL LLAND
JUANITA
LONDOÑO–GAVIRIA
ARCTURUS

Arcturus

This edition published in 2025 by Arcturus Publishing Limited
26/27 Bickels Yard, 151–153 Bermondsey Street,
London SE1 3HA

Writers: Dr. Michael Leach and Dr. Meriel Lland
Illustrator: Juanita Londoño-Gaviria
Designer: Rosie Bellwood
Editors: Becca Clunes, Felicity Forster, and Lydia Halliday
Managing Editor: Joe Harris
Managing Designer: Georgina Wood

ISBN: 978-1-3988-3118-6
CH011053US
Supplier 29, Date 0225, PI 00009225

Printed in China

CHARLES DARWIN'S

On the ORIGIN of SPECIES

INTRODUCTION

ABOUT DARWIN

DARWIN'S KEY THEORIES

DARWIN'S LEGACY

SCIENCE TODAY

INTRODUCTION

WHAT IS EVOLUTION?

We live in an ever-changing world. Our landscapes—the rocks, mountains, valleys, seas, and shorelines—all change shape over long periods of time. People and species of plants and animals also change bit by bit over many generations. These processes are gradual and are the basis of evolution—or how living things change over time.

Evolution is the way that living things here on Earth have changed and continue to change.

Evolution ensures that successful plants and animals "fit"—or are adapted to—their surroundings or environments.

Evolution explains why there are so many different kinds of plants and animals.

Evolution also helps us to understand how groups of animals and plants became extinct, and how new groups emerged—including humans.

Darwin's Ground-Breaking Book

People have not always thought that our planet and living things are in a process of constant change. As recently as 200 years ago, the world was believed to be a much more fixed and stable place. Then, in 1859, Charles Darwin published his book *On the Origin of Species by Means of Natural Selection*, often abbreviated to *Origin*. His book helped us to rethink how, over time, new kinds of living things come into being—or evolve—while others die out. *Origin* explains that evolution takes place through the mechanism of "natural selection."

Darwin says that living things are born with small differences—or variations. Those with differences that make them best adapted to their environment survive, thrive, and reproduce, while those that are less well adapted die out. This is the process of natural selection.

In this book, we explore how *Origin* explains evolution and natural selection, how they work, how they were discovered, and what they mean for scientists today.

PAVING THE WAY FOR DARWIN

Many scientists and thinkers proposed their own ideas about geology and evolution in the eighteenth and nineteenth centuries. Darwin was born into an intellectual world full of questions and theories that had an influence on *Origin*.

Jean-Baptiste Lamarck

In 1809, French biologist Jean-Baptiste Lamarck was the first person to publish a comprehensive theory of evolution. He believed living things could change in their own lifetimes, then pass those changes on to their offspring. For example, a person could lift weights in the gym to become super strong, and their children would inherit that same strength. Although now proven incorrect, Lamarck's ideas helped Darwin to focus on how change actually happened.

Erasmus Darwin

Darwin's grandfather, Erasmus, published *Zoonomia* in 1794, in which he suggested that warm-blooded animals may share a common origin. He also suggested that living things changed over time—starting with plants, then animals. Darwin found these ideas interesting, but thought the book lacked hard facts to support the theories.

Mary Anning

Famous fossil hunter Mary Anning lived and worked in Lyme Regis, on the coast of England. She discovered many important fossilized remains that helped other scientists think about how living things were different in the past. She often worked accompanied by her dog, Tray.

James Hutton

The father of modern geology, James Hutton, developed the theory that geological features underwent constant, super-slow transformations. He may have inspired Darwin to consider that plants and animals changed similarly slowly.

Leclerc de Buffon

One of the most widely read naturalists of his time, Leclerc de Buffon developed theories on the history of the Earth, and about reproduction. Darwin said Buffon was "the first author who in modern times has treated ... [evolution] in a scientific spirit."

Robert Edmond Grant and Charles Lyell

In the late 1820s, scientists Robert Edmond Grant and Charles Lyell made two important suggestions about life on Earth: First, that all living things could change into new species; and second, that plants and animals shared a common origin. They used evidence from geological records to formulate their ideas, but didn't know how these changes might have occurred. Darwin read Lyell's *Principles of Geology* during his travels on HMS *Beagle*.

ABOUT DARWIN

WHO WAS CHARLES DARWIN?

Charles Robert Darwin is considered one of the greatest scientists the world has ever known. In his famous book of 1859, *On the Origin of Species by Means of Natural Selection*, he gave an account of how species develop and change over time. This is the theory of evolution by natural selection, and it changed how we understand the diversity of life on Earth forever.

Seashells in Scotland

In 1825, aged 16, Darwin began to study medicine at Edinburgh University. He didn't enjoy his classes, however, and spent most of his time exploring the outdoors and gathering specimens for his natural history collection. He especially liked collecting seashells for examination. Eventually it was decided that he would leave medicine and change direction.

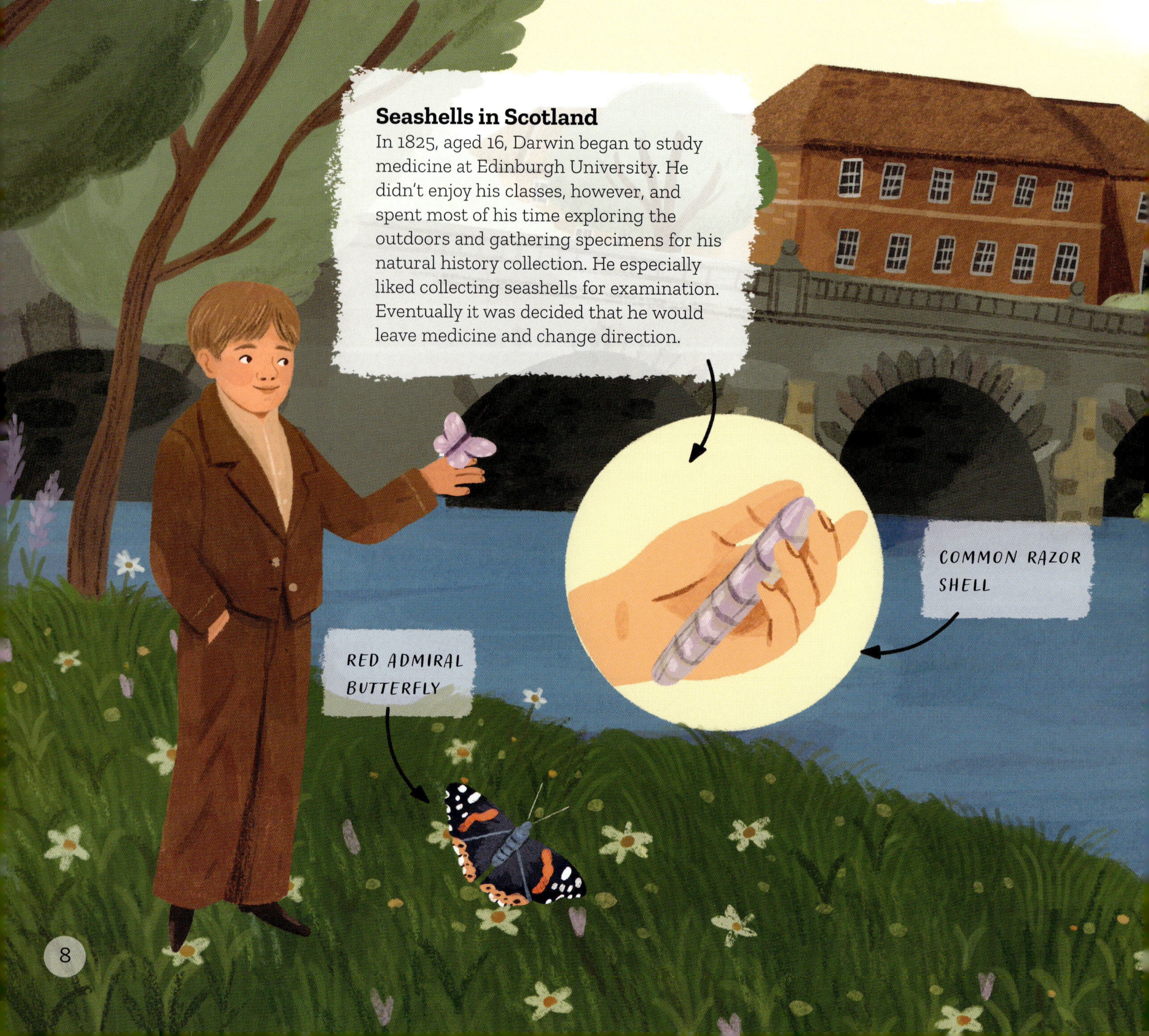

Darwin was born in Shrewsbury, England, on February 12, 1809. His father, Robert, was a doctor, and his mother, Susanna, was the daughter of a famous china manufacturer, Josiah Wedgwood. The Darwins lived in a house called "The Mount," on the banks of the river Severn. Darwin wasn't a great student in school, but he loved exploring the natural world and learning from first-hand experience of nature.

"Beetling" at Cambridge

In 1828, Darwin began studying at Christ's College, Cambridge, to become a minister in the Anglican Church. His special hobby at that time was "beetling"—competitively collecting and preserving specimens of beetles. At one point, when Darwin had collected two rare bugs, he spotted a third. Trying to free up a hand to capture it, he popped one of the other ground beetles into his mouth. The bug released a foul-tasting fluid that burned his tongue, and Darwin had to spit it out. Spluttering and coughing, he lost his prize!

DARWIN IN THE GALÁPAGOS

After university, Darwin found his perfect job as a naturalist on board the HMS *Beagle*. The volcanic Galápagos Islands are 1,000 km (620 miles) from the coast of South America. When he arrived there, Darwin was 22 years old. In the four years he had been at sea, his skill as a naturalist had improved considerably. His huge collection of specimens now included plants, animals, and fossils.

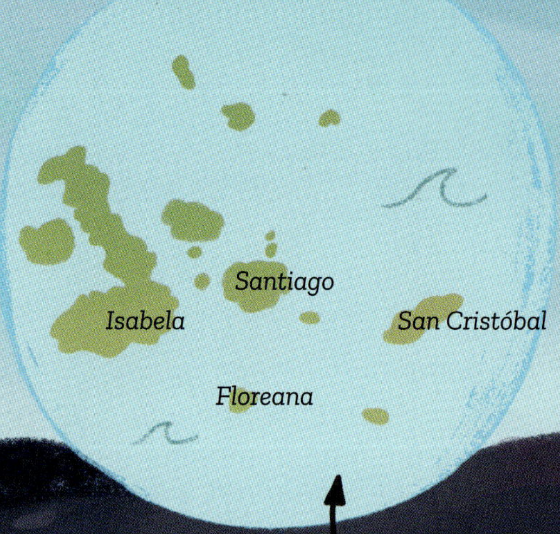

There are more than 100 Galápagos islands, although some of them are tiny. Darwin landed on four of the islands.

Galápagos Tortoise (*Chelonoidis nigra*)
Giant tortoises on the islands had two very different shell shapes: some were domed, while others were shaped like a saddle. Darwin saw that the different forms gave the tortoises advantages in obtaining different kinds of foods in their environment. These variations, and the advantages they offer, are important features of natural selection.

SALLY LIGHTFOOT CRABS

SEA LIONS

Darwin's Finches
There are 13 species of finch on the Galápagos Islands, all small and quite similar in appearance. Later, these birds became important to Darwin's understanding of adaptation. The birds show great diversity in their beaks, feeding habits, and habitats. Some finches are insectivores, some eat grains, others fruit or large seeds. They helped Darwin to illustrate how species evolve over time.

Arriving in the Galápagos

On September 15, 1835, HMS *Beagle* arrived at San Cristóbal Island, and Darwin began to study the local wildlife. At first, he did not bother to keep good records, assuming that the same species would be found on all of the Galápagos Islands. However, he soon discovered just how wrong he was!

"I never dreamed that islands, about fifty or sixty miles apart, and most of them in sight of each other, formed of precisely the same rocks, placed under a quite similar climate, rising to a nearly equal height, would have been differently tenanted; but we shall soon see that this is the case."

Charles Darwin, in his book *The Voyage of the* Beagle (1891).

Exploring the Islands

Wildlife on the islands showed little fear of people, and Darwin had closer encounters with nature than ever before. He spent five weeks exploring the islands—making records and collecting specimens. His biggest ideas were born from questions raised here.

DARWIN AND WALLACE

Back home in England, Darwin married and moved to Down House. There, he began to write about his travels and observations. He shared his discoveries with other scientists, and continued to experiment to test out his ideas. Darwin liked to walk as he thought. He had a circular walk called the Sandwalk or "thinking path" laid in the gardens, and walked it with his dogs several times each day.

Family Life
Emma Wedgwood, who was Darwin's first cousin, became his wife in January 1839. They had 10 children and made their busy home at Down House.

The Grand Idea

Darwin believed there were always small "variations"—or differences—between members of the same species, which could be passed from parent to offspring. Some of these variations were useful and might help the offspring to be better adapted to the environment—to have better eyesight and find more food, for example. The better-adapted animals lived longer and had more offspring, to whom they passed on their useful traits. Over a very long time, these traits became normal for the whole population. This idea is evolution through natural selection.

Two Great Minds

Alfred Russel Wallace, a British surveyor and teacher, was also a keen collector of plants and animals. He had been traveling widely in South America and South East Asia and, by 1856, was discussing evolution in letters with Darwin. In 1858, while in Asia, he struck upon a similar understanding of how species change—natural selection. He sent this idea to Darwin, and the two wrote a joint paper for presentation in the same year.

Darwin's Delay

Darwin was determined to gather as much evidence and as many examples as possible to support his theories. He was concerned about how his ideas would be received by his fellow scientists and by wider society. It was only after 16 years of thought and experiment that he finally decided to go public. He was prompted to do so by the work of Wallace.

LIGHTING A FIRE

In 1858, Darwin and Wallace's theory of natural selection was first presented at a scientific meeting in London. Both men acknowledged that Darwin was the first to outline the theory, but it was not until a year later that *Origin* was published and Darwin became truly famous.

ORIGIN, PUBLISHED IN 1859

AN EARLY MICROSCOPE

All Change

The 1800s were a time of great change in science. There were many new inventions, one of which was the steam train. This was also a period when people began to explore the past, digging up fossils, and excavating the remains of ancient civilizations. Scientists were learning more about how Earth had changed over time. The publication of *Origin* threw Britain into a whirl of excitement. Almost everyone had an opinion about the book. Some rejected the ideas; others believed the radical theory to be correct. In particular, evolution was seen as a challenge to the Christian Church, which taught that all things were made by God.

Did life begin in the Garden of Eden, as the Bible explains? Were animals saved on Noah's Ark? How did different species appear?

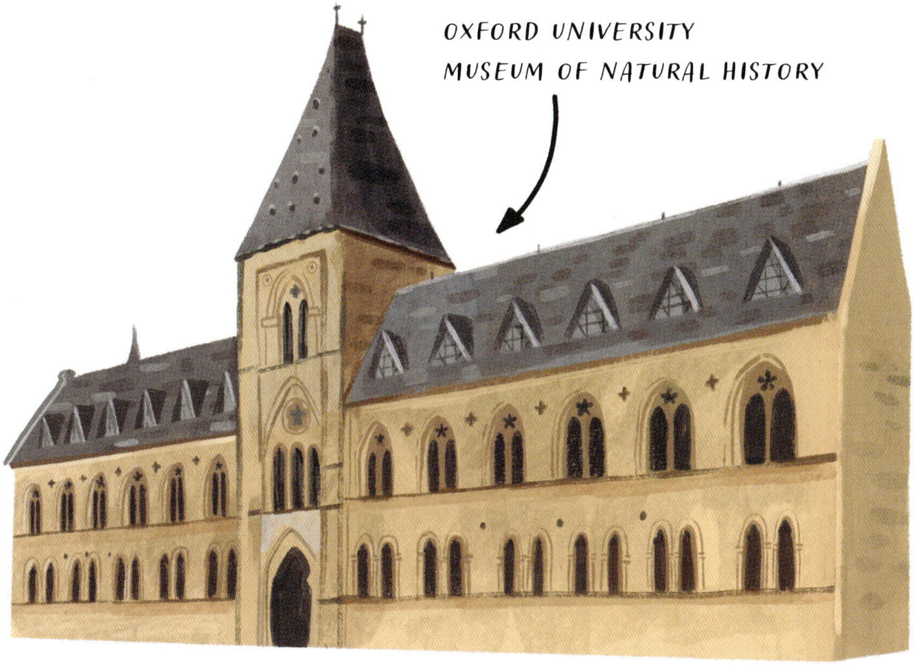

The Debate

In June 1860, scientists came together for a meeting in Oxford to discuss natural selection. The debate became very heated. Two figures dominated the discussion—Thomas Huxley and Bishop Samuel Wilberforce. Huxley represented the view of science, and Wilberforce the view of the Church. Neither Darwin nor Wallace attended.

Outcomes

Both Huxley and Wilberforce were excellent speakers, and the debate is considered by many to be a key moment in the acceptance of evolution.

One other important reaction to *Origin* came from Alfred Russel Wallace himself. Wallace told Darwin that he didn't think natural selection applied to human beings. Darwin thought otherwise, and this prompted him to start work on a new book—he called it his "Man-book"—which explored the evolution of humans.

The great speakers, Wilberforce (left), and Huxley (right).

The Church-versus-science debate became very heated.

"My book has stirred up the mud."

Charles Darwin, in a letter to Asa Gray (1860).

THE "MAN-BOOK"

Darwin's theory of the evolution of human beings was published in a new book, *The Descent of Man, and Selection in Relation to Sex*, in 1871. The excitement created by *Origin* reached fever pitch with Darwin's "Man-book."

While many people looked to the Bible to explain the emergence of humans in the story of Adam and Eve, Darwin saw humans as part of the animal kingdom, rather than being set apart from it. He believed that people evolved in the same way as other animals, and that humans and apes shared a common ancestor.

Darwin was ridiculed in the popular press, as this cartoon from 1871 shows.

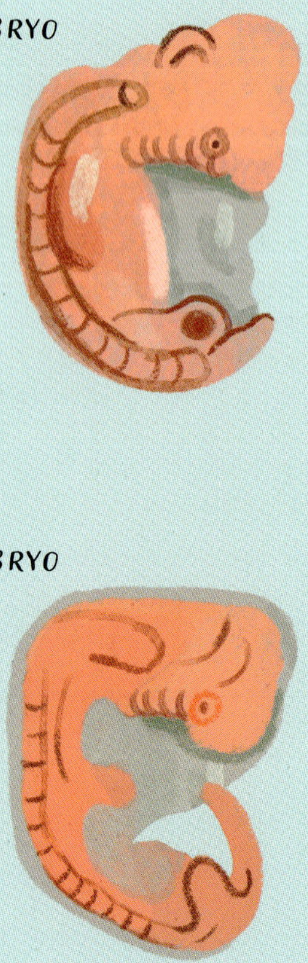

Human and dog embryos show similarities.

Common Ancestor

Darwin said that humans and apes shared a common ancestor. Back in time, the descendants of this ancestor split off into different families of animals. Darwin illustrated the similarity between the human body and the bodies of other mammals. He looked at similarities in their skeletons and also in their embryos—unborn offspring. But human evolution is also about mental traits. Darwin concluded that the brain—just as much as the body—evolved in response to natural selection.

This cartoon from the French newspaper *Figaro* depicts Darwin showing a monkey its reflection.

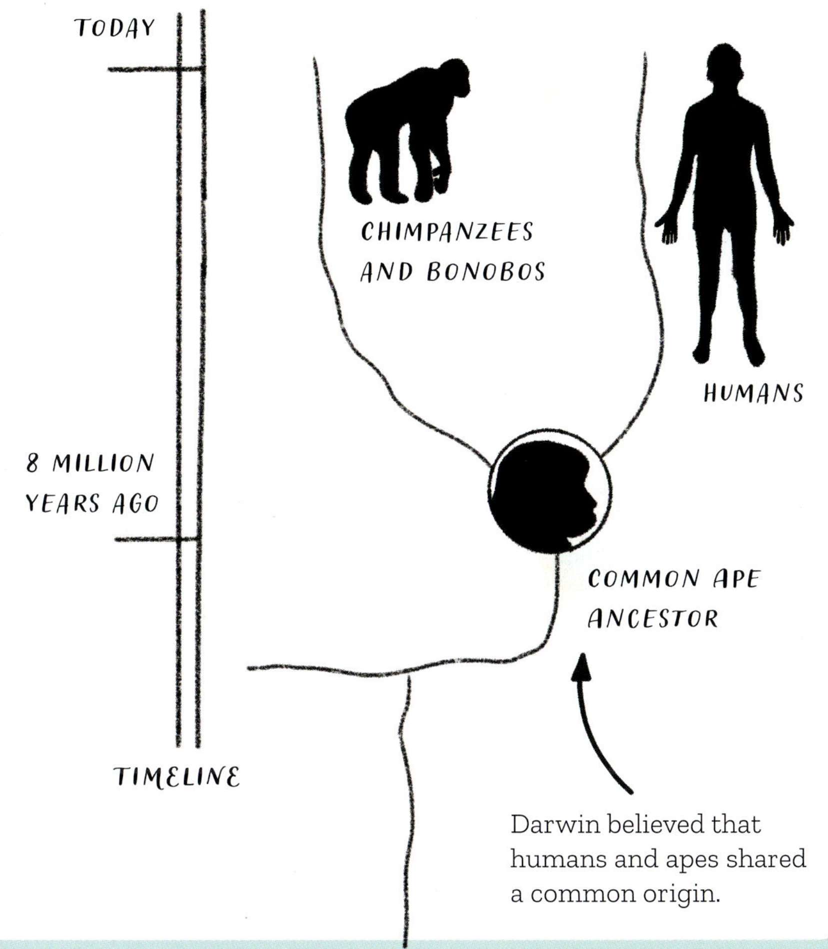

Darwin believed that humans and apes shared a common origin.

"Man still bears in his bodily frame the indelible stamp of his lowly origin."

Charles Darwin, *The Descent of Man* (1871)

Sexual Selection

In addition to the theory of natural selection, Darwin introduced the idea of "sexual selection." It's called this because in some species an individual is selected as a mate based on certain traits. For example, male deer might battle each other to show who is strongest and win the right to mate with females. Or a female bird might choose a male with the most complex song. Such traits boost reproduction, but can also hinder survival as fighting males risk injury and singing birds become a target for predators.

Usually only the healthiest animals get to mate and pass on their characteristics. Both natural selection and sexual selection involve traits being passed on to offspring. This enables species to change over time.

The complex song of the male wren encourages a mate.

AN EXPERIMENTAL LIFE

Darwin never stopped learning or experimenting. He retained his scientist's passion for investigation and observation. He regularly communicated with a global network of "pen-pals"—over 2,000—with whom he tested out ideas about life on Earth. He wrote 14 books, four monographs on single species, and exchanged over 15,000 letters.

In his letters, Darwin shared his ideas with many scientists.

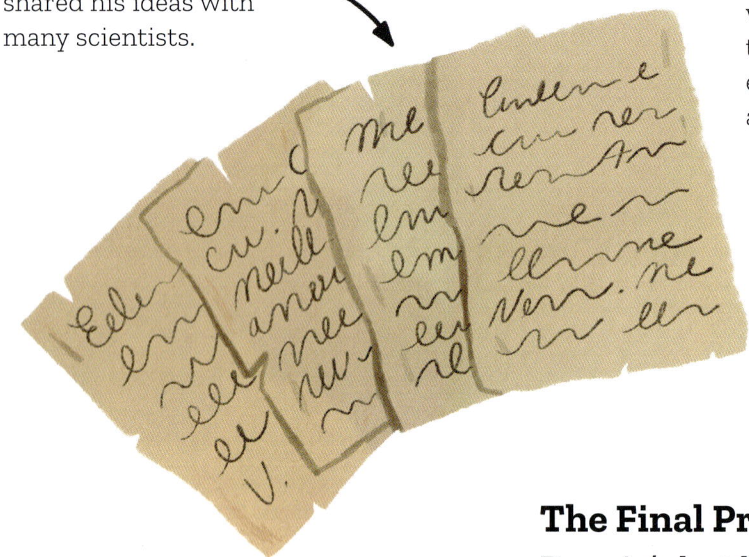

Darwin spent his whole adult life thinking, walking, experimenting, and writing.

The Final Project

Darwin's last book was called *The Formation of Vegetable Mould, through the Action of Worms, with Observations on their Habits*, published in 1881, just six months before his death. It documents around 50 years of exploring how earthworms function, and their contribution to the ecosystem (the community of living things in an environment).

This cartoon of the time makes fun of Darwin, showing him with an earthworm as a question mark.

Darwin persuaded family, friends, and colleagues to help in his experiments. Could worms hear? Darwin's children played piano and bassoon to the creatures. They shouted at the worms and noted responses. Worm casts were collected from all around Britain and beyond. The book revealed the volume of earth raised to the surface by worms each year, and it showed how worms improve soil, help crops grow, and, literally, move the earth under our feet.

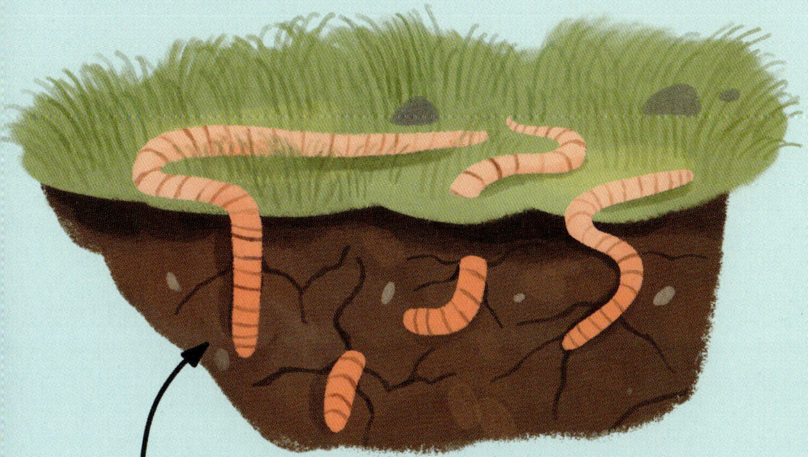

Earthworms feeding on, and improving, the soil.

Darwin Unearths How Earthworms Work

Earthworms live in soil and leaf litter. As they burrow, they consume soil, feeding on decomposing organic matter such as leaves. They then poop out their worm casts, bringing nutrients to the surface and maintaining soil health. To the very end of his life, Darwin made important discoveries such as this, that changed how we view the world around us.

Celebration of Life

Darwin died in 1882. He was given a prestigious burial in Westminster Abbey, London. Darwin has been celebrated worldwide in the naming of over 250 species. One of them is the remarkable Darwin's frog (*Rhinoderma darwinii*), the only male frog to brood its young in a vocal pouch—an exciting example of how unlikely natural selection can be!

DARWIN'S GRAVE AT WESTMINSTER ABBEY

This statue of Darwin has pride of place in the Natural History Museum, London.

Darwin's frog is a species as remarkable as its namesake.

DARWIN'S KEY THEORIES

MYSTERIOUS EVOLUTION

Earth is brimming with life. From the depths of the oceans to the rain forest canopy, plants and animals thrive. Travel back in time, and the world would look very different. How Earth became a planet humming with diverse life is down to the processes of evolution.

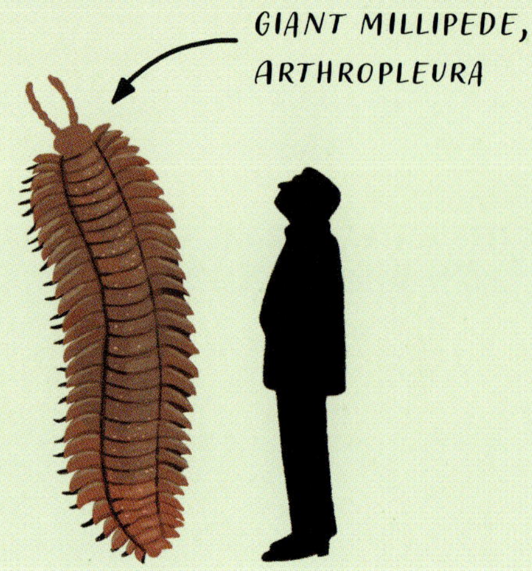

Could a millipede be taller than a human?

Evidence for Natural Selection

Using his vast specimen collection, as well as his observations of living and fossilized plants and animals, Darwin theorized that living things were controlled by what he called "natural selection." The big idea here is that the most successful animals and plants were those best adapted to their environment. Others died out.

Fossil Finds—Mighty Millipedes

Fossils can show some of the ways in which things change over time. Today, the African giant black millipede can grow to 36 cm (15 in) long—huge compared to its many thumbnail-sized relatives. But this is tiny next to *Arthropleura*, a fossilized giant millipede, 2.7 m (8.9 ft) long, from around 350 million years ago. It seems that much smaller millipedes were able to survive, while their giant ancestors could not. Perhaps something in their environment, the climate, or food sources changed, causing *Arthropleura* to die out.

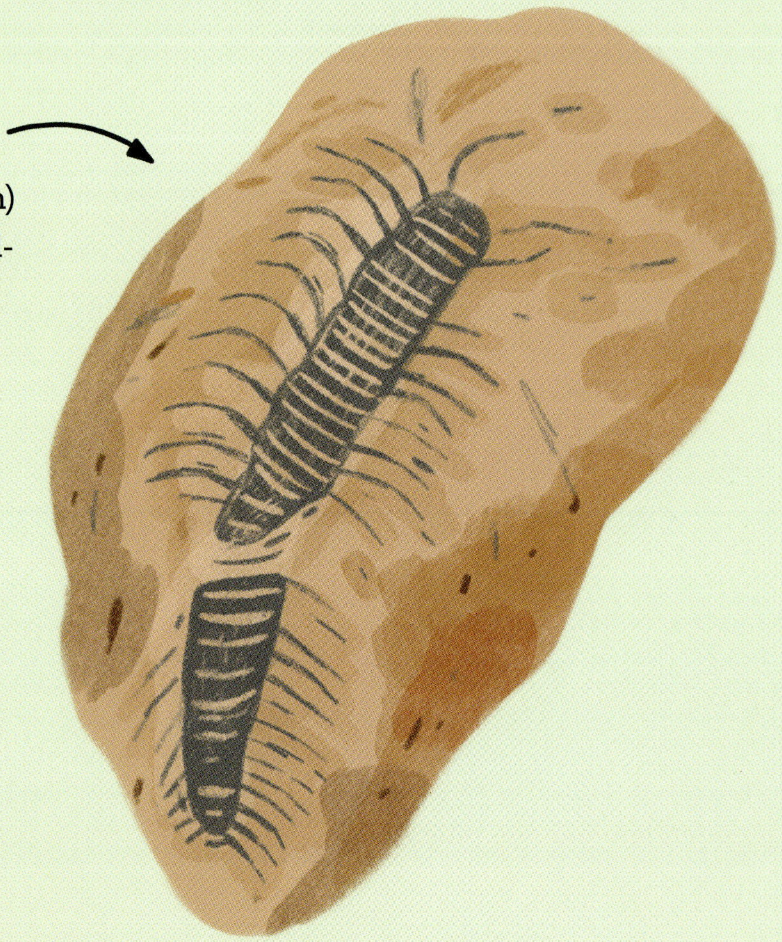

Incomplete Fossil Record

Fossils are the preserved remains or traces of animals and plants that lived millions of years ago. They are formed in very special circumstances—for example, when an animal dies and is quickly covered by sediment such as sand, mud, or volcanic ash. Since these circumstances happen rarely, and few are uncovered, the fossil record of life on Earth is incomplete. We have discovered fossils for less than 1 percent of the animals that have ever lived. The other 99 percent are unknown to us. Attempting to work out exactly how one animal evolved is like trying to solve a 500-piece jigsaw puzzle when 450 pieces are missing!

Some animals have died out. Darwin discovered the fossilized jaw of the extinct giant ground sloth, or mylodon.

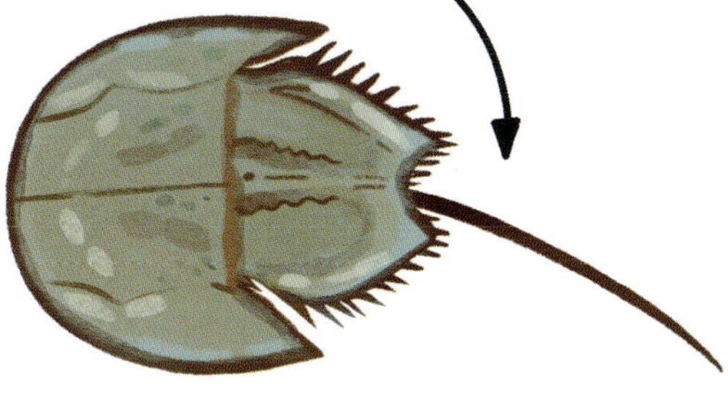

Some animals have survived for millennia. The horseshoe crab, for example, has changed very little in 480 million years. We call these "living fossils." This is because they are so perfectly adapted to their environment that they no longer need to evolve.

VARIATION IN ACTION

A species is a group of plants or animals that are similar in appearance and can breed together to produce fertile offspring. Darwin tried to understand why there were so many species on Earth, whether those species were different in the past, and how living things changed from one form to another.

Natural selection—the way in which the most well-adapted living things survive—relies on differences or "variations" between individuals. These variations can be helpful or unhelpful in terms of a species' survival. Useful variations mean a species will thrive and pass on advantages to their offspring. Let's look at variation in action.

A Frog's Story

Imagine frogs living on the ground in the rainforests of southern Thailand. The frogs have a range of head shapes, skin tones, and textures.

Life on the Forest Floor

The frogs live in damp, cool leaf litter. They hunt spiders, lizards, and small rodents at night. At the same time, the frogs are hunted by snakes and birds.

The brownish, patterned frogs with angular leaf-shaped heads are well camouflaged. This enables them to avoid predators and catch more prey. As a result, they live longer and have more babies, passing on their physical features to their young.

Best Disguise

Over time and many generations, the most successful frogs are those that most closely resemble their surroundings. Meet the long-nosed horned frog (*Pelobatrachus nasutus*), or leaf frog.

The leaf frog is very distinctive against a light background in daylight ...

... but is almost impossible to see among the leaf litter.

TAMING THE WILD

Humans have taken advantage of the variations that occur within a species by encouraging selective breeding, which is sometimes called "artificial breeding." Humans select the characteristics or traits in a plant or animal that they want to carry into the next generation. For example, early farmers selectively bred food crops, like wheat and barley, for higher yields and greater disease resistance. Darwin studied the selective breeding of cattle, sheep, and dogs.

GREAT DANE AND CHIHUAHUA

From titan to tiny, Great Danes and Chihuahuas are actually part of the same species.

On the Farm

Humans began to farm plants and animals around 10,000 years ago. Over thousands of years, farmers changed many plant species by collecting seeds from those with traits they needed. Wild cabbages have been selectively bred to produce many different forms, such as cauliflower and broccoli. Tomatoes, apples, lentils, and peas were all once wild plants that have been changed by human selection.

FROM WOLF TO WOOF!

The origin of the dog goes back to the gray wolf. Around 25,000 years ago, humans began to interact with wild wolves. The most friendly of the wolves became regular visitors to human settlements and slowly came to offer protection in return for food. Humans began to selectively breed wolf cubs for particular traits such as loyalty or a steady temperament. Humans also looked at physical traits—by choosing particularly tall females to mate with tall males, tall puppies were born. Other characteristics were chosen to make the animals smaller, stronger, or faster. We now have a wide variety of dogs with different strengths.

FROM ONE COME MANY

"Common descent" is a term that describes how a group of organisms can share a common ancestor. *Origin* explained that within one species, many breeds might evolve. The example Darwin used to demonstrate this was the domestic pigeon.

Wild rock pigeons were the first birds to be domesticated by humans. In the Middle East, more than 5,000 years ago, they were caught and bred for meat and eggs. Whenever people moved to new areas, they took their birds along with them, and soon pigeons could be found in most parts of the world.

Pigeon breeding became a popular hobby, and people started selectively choosing birds to produce new forms. There were soon varieties of pigeons with curled feathers or collars. Darwin bred his own pigeons to test his theories. He learned that they often passed on their tail shape or the shade of their feathers to their chicks. Pigeon breeding helped Darwin understand that evolution by selection really worked.

"Great as the differences are between the breeds of pigeons, I am fully convinced that the common opinion of naturalists is correct, namely, that all have descended from the rock pigeon."

Charles Darwin, in his book *On the Origin of Species* (1859)

Coo of the Wild

Pigeons are not always easy to keep captive. Many farmed birds escaped into the wild and started to breed. Once free to select their own mates, the pigeons started to change their appearance again. They began to look less like fancy breeds and more like their rock pigeon ancestors. These eventually became the wild city pigeons that we now see around the world.

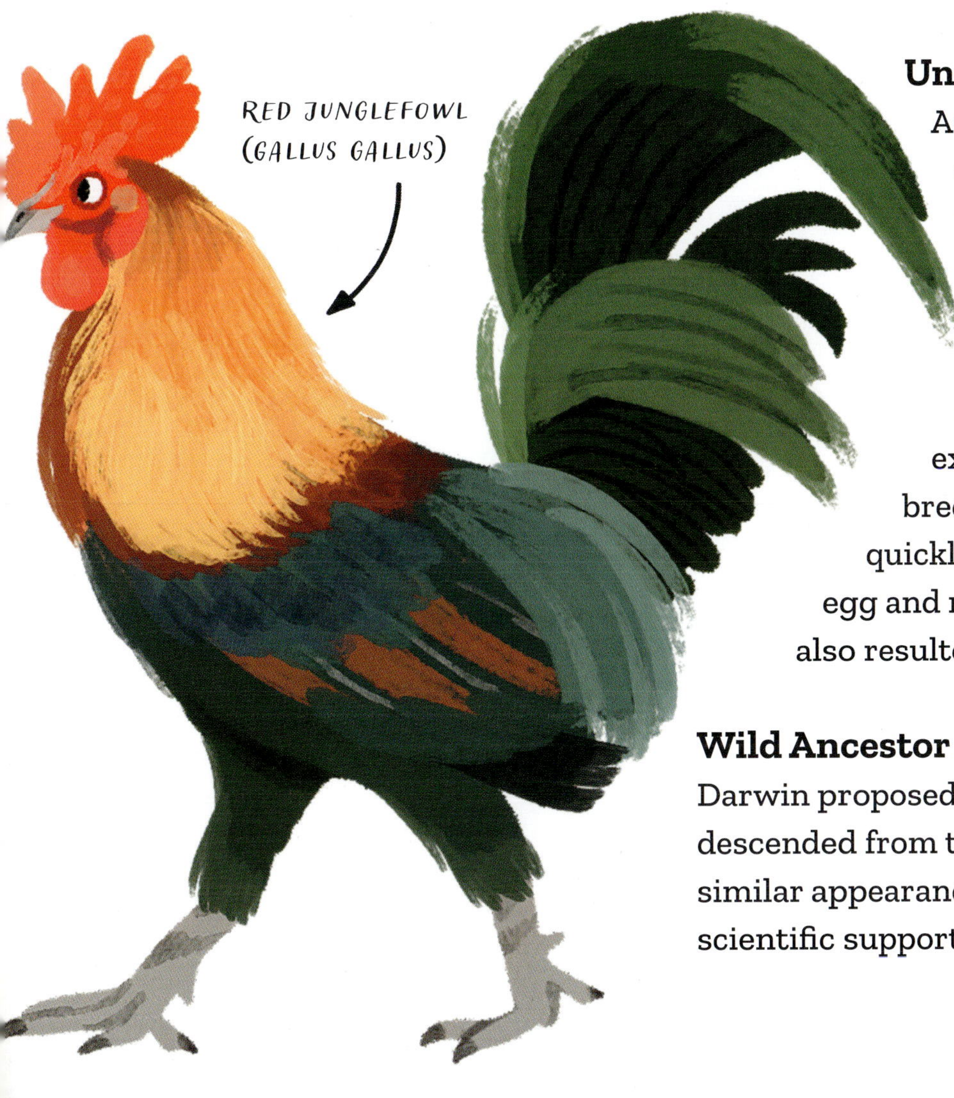

Unconscious Selection

As with the wolf or the pigeon, descendants can show different variations that humans select for breeding. But not all selection is conscious. Alongside one particular difference, other—sometimes invisible—differences might exist. For example, humans have selectively bred domestic chickens to mature more quickly than their wild ancestors to enable egg and meat production. But this process has also resulted in smaller leg bones and brain size.

Wild Ancestor

Darwin proposed that domestic chickens were descended from the red junglefowl because of their similar appearance. Modern DNA research has given scientific support to his theory.

SURVIVAL OF THE FITTEST

Have you ever heard the phrase "survival of the fittest?" In later editions of *Origin*, Darwin uses this term to describe the mechanism that underpins natural selection. Here "fittest" does not mean the strongest or fastest. Instead, it means the species that are best "fitted" to their environment. The best-adapted plants or animals will be the ones to survive and reproduce.

Galápagos Islands

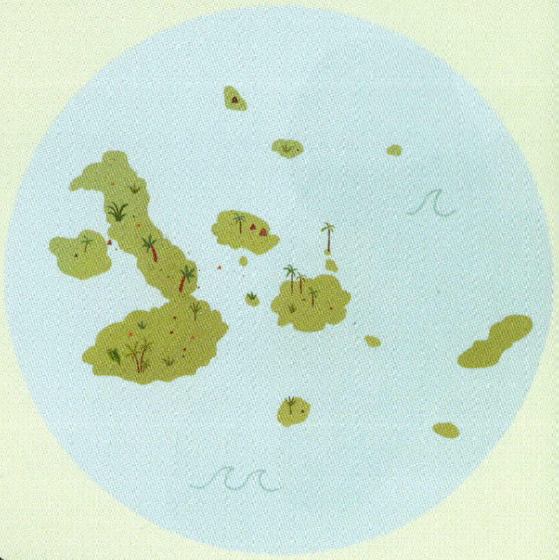

"I have called this principle, by which each slight variation, if useful, is preserved, by the term Natural Selection ... But the expression often used by Mr. Herbert Spencer of the Survival of the Fittest is more accurate ..."

Charles Darwin, *On the Origin of Species* (1859)

Darwin's Finches

One of Darwin's most important discoveries was made following his travels to the Galápagos Islands. Using specimens collected there, he was able to see that one group of birds—the finches—appeared to be very similar to each other, except for the shape of their beaks. Natural selection, or the survival of the fittest, helps to explain their story.

History of the Finches

Around 2 million years ago, small birds—grassquits—were blown 965 km (600 miles) across the sea from South America to the Galápagos Islands. Each island offered different food sources. The birds evolved variations in beak shape and size to adapt to their new homes. For example, on rocky islands with lots of insects, long, slim beaks were an advantage for probing between stones to dig out bugs. The long-beaked birds fed well and had many young—passing on their useful beak shape.

Elsewhere, forested islands offered lots of seeds. To open their hard shells, birds needed the advantage of especially wide and powerful beaks. These powerful beaks slowly evolved into those of the large ground finches that crack open big seeds today. This explains how useful variations within a species come to feature in most of the population.

GRAY WARBLER-FINCH (CERTHIDEA FUSCA)

The gray warbler-finches of Pinta Island have a slender beak.

LARGE GROUND FINCH (GEOSPIZA MAGNIROSTRIS)

The large ground finches have a very different beak.

Gruesome but True

There is little fresh water to be found on some islands. Because of this shortage, a few strong-billed finches learned to drink blood! The vampire ground finches peck holes in the skin of seabirds.

VAMPIRE GROUND FINCH (GEOSPIZA SEPTENTRIONALIS)

Special Finch Tricks

Super smart and slender-billed woodpecker finches use cactus spines to dig out grubs from holes in wood.

WOODPECKER FINCH (CAMARHYNCHUS PALLIDUS)

STRUGGLE FOR EXISTENCE

Darwin wrote about the "struggle for life," where whole species or individual animals have to compete for territory and food because there is a limited supply of these essentials. He believed that the animals that were best adapted to their habitat would survive and breed. The species that failed to adapt would become extinct.

Mammoth Challenge

Woolly mammoths first appeared nearly one million years ago. Their thick coats protected them from the cold temperatures of the Ice Age, when land in the northern hemisphere was covered with glaciers and ice fields. Around 12,000 years ago, the landscape grew warmer—too warm for the mammoths' heavy coats. At the same time, other animals moved up from the south—species that were better suited to the warming climate. Finally, humans arrived to hunt these slow-moving giants. Mammoths became extinct around 8,000 years ago, because they could not adapt quickly enough to the changing conditions, or avoid predatory humans.

Ice Baby

In 2012, a frozen baby woolly mammoth was found in the Siberian tundra. It was around 30,000 years old, and has helped us to understand more about the species.

The Heavy Mob

About 15 million years ago, the ancestors of today's penguins could fly. They ate fish and competed with other seabirds to find food on the ocean surface. Some of the heavier birds found food by diving deeper into the water. They put on weight to help them dive. This made flying more difficult but provided more food, so their extra size was passed on to their young.

Underwater "Flight"

Penguins evolved in a landscape with no land predators, and before long they had no need to fly at all. Their wings became fins to power them through water as they hunted. They evolved thick layers of fat to keep out the cold. Evolution has produced birds that are perfectly adapted to their habitat.

SEXUAL SELECTION

After years of research, Darwin realized that some animals had adaptations that could not be explained by the struggle to find food or escape enemies. He believed that some species were changed by the competition for mates. All animals have an instinct to mate and breed, and the most successful pass on their characteristics to the next generation. Certain "variations"—or differences—such as antlers, plumage, song, movements, and strength—can prove very attractive to mates.

Fabulous Fairywrens

Small birds face many predators, and one of the best defenses is to stay hidden. For most of the year, male superb fairywrens in Australia are a dull brown, perfect for camouflage in their undergrowth habitat. But during the breeding season, males need to compete and advertise their suitability to females. The males lose their brown appearance and grow an amazing set of bright blue feathers. Females choose the most vibrant males as mates. Males with dull plumage usually don't get the chance to breed.

Size Matters

Bull (male) elephant seals are huge—they weigh around eight to ten times more than females. The largest bulls can grow to 6 m (20 ft) in length and weigh up to 4,000 kg (9,000 lb). This big size difference between males and females is called extreme sexual dimorphism.

Only the largest bulls get to breed. Smaller males are attacked and driven away. The big males pass on their vast size to their male young, and over thousands of years they keep getting bigger and bigger.

Sexual dimorphism in elephant seals means that the bulls are much larger than the cows (females).

A bull fight.

Over Here!

Female fiddler crabs have two identical small front claws, while the lopsided males have one small claw and one huge claw. When looking for a mate, a male waves his giant claw in the air with gusto, signaling that he is strong and healthy. Females choose to mate with the male with the biggest claw. In the process, males with smaller claws have slowly died out, while other crabs have claws that get bigger over the generations.

The waving display attracts females and can also result in duels between males.

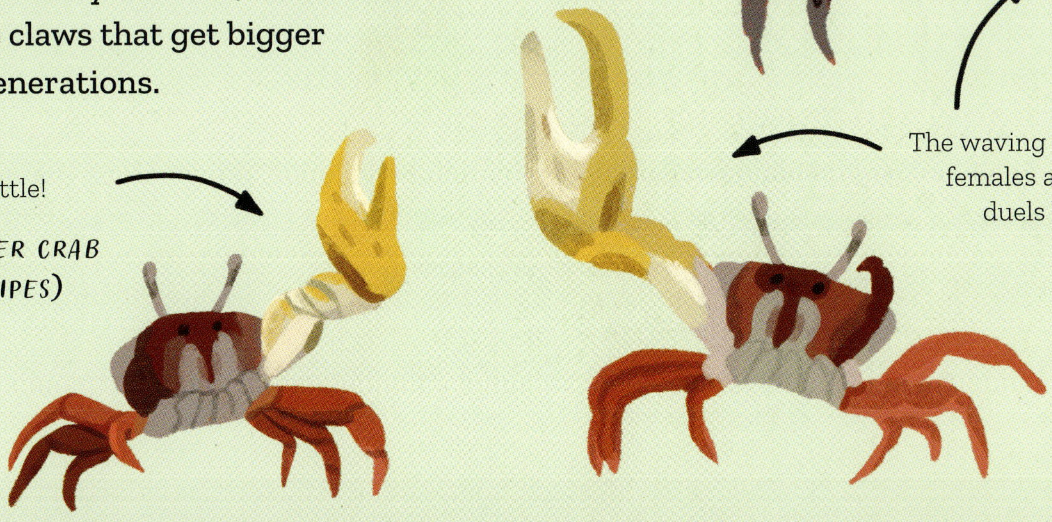

A big claw battle!

MALE FIDDLER CRAB (UCA ANNULIPES)

INSTINCT AND HABITS IN ANIMALS

Fossils can help us understand how animals change and adapt over time. But physical evolution is only part of the story. Darwin saw instinct and habits as equally important in natural selection—but they leave few traces. Just like animals' bodies, animal habits have also evolved over millions of years, passing on from adults to young.

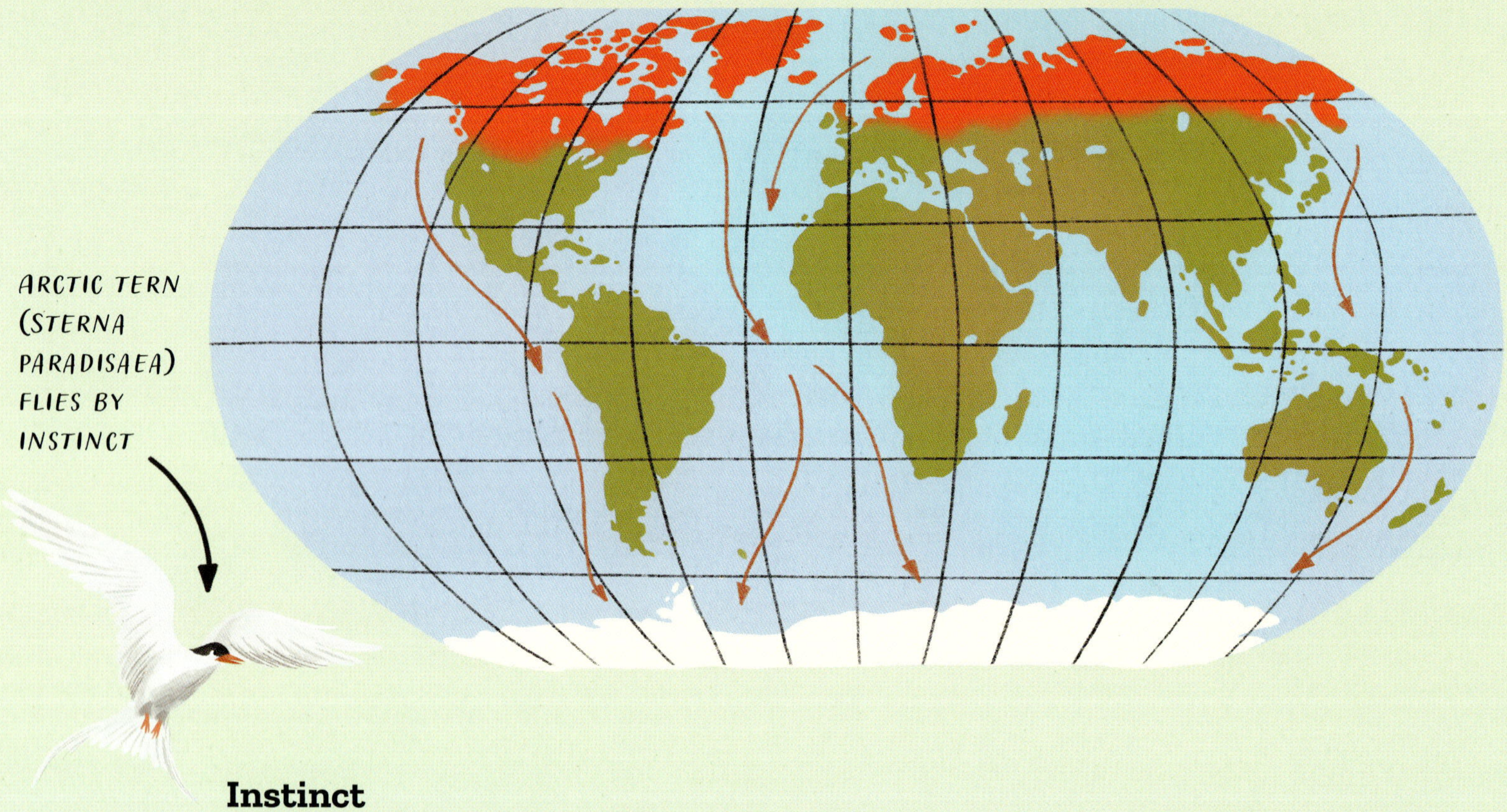

Instinct

Instinct within a species is when all individuals do the same things without having to learn how to do them. Individuals perform instinctive actions without understanding why they do so. Darwin decided that if an instinct helped survival, it would be passed on to offspring, and ultimately to the whole species.

Migrants by Nature

Arctic terns constantly travel. They fly around 90,000 km (56,000 miles) every year entirely by instinct. Migration probably started during the last Ice Age. When the seas became frozen, the birds were forced to move south so they could continue to catch fish. Some went as far as the Antarctic. When weather in the Antarctic becomes super cold, the terns fly north to their breeding grounds. When the northern winter begins they return south. They migrate in order to breed, and instinct drives them to make this incredible journey twice each year.

EGG-EATING SNAKES (DASYPELTIS SCABRA) HUNT OUT THE EGGS OF BIRDS LAID ON THE GROUND OR IN TREES

Nest Builders

Birds are not taught to build nests by their parents; they make them by instinct. The first birds probably laid eggs directly on the ground. Gradually, some began to cover their eggs with leaves to hide them from predators, and more eggs hatched. Hiding eggs was a useful variation in the way birds behaved, because it helped more chicks to survive. Soon, eggs were laid on twig platforms built in trees away from ground predators. Even more chicks survived. Over millions of years, birds evolved better nests. Penduline tits build nests of spider web, animal hair, and leaves above water, making them difficult for predators to reach.

EURASIAN PENDULINE TIT (REMIZ PENDULINUS) NEST WITH YOUNG

ISLAND LIFE

Darwin's understanding of evolution was inspired in large part by his time on the Galápagos Islands. Small islands offer very special circumstances for their inhabitants. Because islands are cut off from the rest of the world, fewer animals can invade, and there is less competition for food and territory. That way, useful variations in a species can arise more quickly, leading to some extraordinary examples of extreme evolution.

Bird Giants

In general, the larger an animal is, the greater advantage it has in the search for food, in what Darwin called the "struggle for life." Meet the elephant bird, once found on the island of Madagascar. Elephant birds were flightless and stood 3 m (10 ft) high, weighing 730 kg (1,600 lb).

Elephant birds evolved to this huge size because the island had no big cats or other large predators to hunt them, and there was little competition for food. This is called "island gigantism." The largest predator on Madagascar was the fossa, which was only 70–80 cm (28–31 in) long and weighed between 5.5 and 8.6 kg (12 and 19 lb). It was large enough to take small elephant bird chicks, but little more.

Arrival of the Egg Hunters

Elephant bird eggs were massive, protected by strong shells that animal scavengers could not open. About 10,000 years ago, humans arrived on the island and had to adapt to the new habitat. Adult elephant birds were too big to be hunted by people, but their huge eggs could be opened with sharp stone tools. Just one egg provided enough food for a small family. Hundreds of thousands of eggs were taken, which had a terrible impact on the elephant bird population.

Evolution usually happens over millions of years, but when a new species arrives in any habitat, the existing animals have to adapt or die out. The elephant birds could not change quickly enough. Their numbers declined, and they became extinct around 1,000 years ago.

A huge elephant bird egg would feed many more people than a chicken's egg.

DARWIN'S LEGACY

FILLING OUT THE FOSSIL TIMELINE

Darwin's *Origin* introduced the world to the process of evolution. But discoveries since its publication have helped scientists to develop an understanding of how evolution shapes the world.

The Fossil Record

Darwin developed his ideas with very little fossil evidence. Most of the world's key fossils had yet to be discovered. Scientists can now fill in some gaps in the evolution timeline.

This reconstructed embryo is from a dinosaur fossil that originated at least 66 million years ago.

Dinosaur Data

The word dinosaur means "terrible lizard," and was first used in 1841. We now know that there were hundreds of dinosaur species, ranging from the chicken-sized Aquilops to the giant Supersaurus at 35 m (115 ft) long.

Timelines

Modern technology helps scientists to work out the age of some animal remains, and to understand just how much time evolutionary processes can take. Insects are occasionally caught in amber, a sticky tree resin that hardens like stone. It preserves the animal inside completely unchanged. The oldest known amber insects lived 230 million years ago.

Whales are part of the family called cetaceans, and their closest living relative today is the hippopotamus.

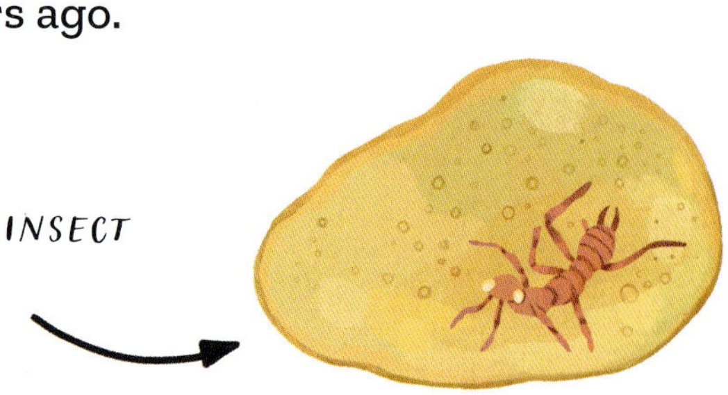

The Story of Whales

Whales were once thought to be strange kinds of fish. But by Darwin's day, people understood that the two were not related—fish breathe in water, while whales need air. Darwin wondered how this difference could have possibly evolved when both animals shared a habitat. He thought whale ancestors might have been insect-eating mammals that lived on the seashore.

Recently discovered fossils show that whales evolved from the deer-like animal Indohyus. Their skeletons suggest that these animals spent some of their life in water. Over a period of 50 million years, they became heavier, changed shape, and moved into the sea. Today's whales are perfectly adapted to water, but still breathe air just like their ancestors.

INDOHYUS

PAKICETUS

AMBULOCETUS

BASILOSAURUS

CETACEA

DARWIN'S TREE OF LIFE

In 1837, Darwin drew a simple doodle in his notebook, with the words "I think" written above. This was an attempt to visually represent the evolution of all life on Earth. It became known as the "Tree of Life," and was the start of one of the biggest ideas in science.

The Tree of Life started out as a doodle in Darwin's notebook.

Darwin's Doodle

In *Origin*, Darwin created a more detailed tree. The trunk of the tree represented the first living creatures, and the top showed animals alive today. Darwin understood that all living creatures evolved from the same ancient ancestors. But since there are around 8 million animal species on Earth, the tree is so complicated that scientists do not fully understand it. In reality, evolution can't be drawn as a simple tree. The first life on Earth was probably bacteria, and from these tiny organisms every other species evolved. But they would have appeared at different times, in different parts of the world.

Darwin's idea was that over time the tree grew bigger—some branches died out, while others extended and split into smaller branches and twigs. If we look back far enough, the tree shows that all species are related.

Evolution of Animals

Darwin's Tree of Life provided an idea of how modern animals evolved. However, tracing the evolution of even one family on the tree is extremely complicated. For example, there are 40 species of wild cats alive today, and many more ancient forms of cat have become extinct. Modern tigers have existed for around 2 million years, but their extinct ancestor, called *Miacis*, is also the ancestor of all wild dogs.

Evolution of the Cat Family

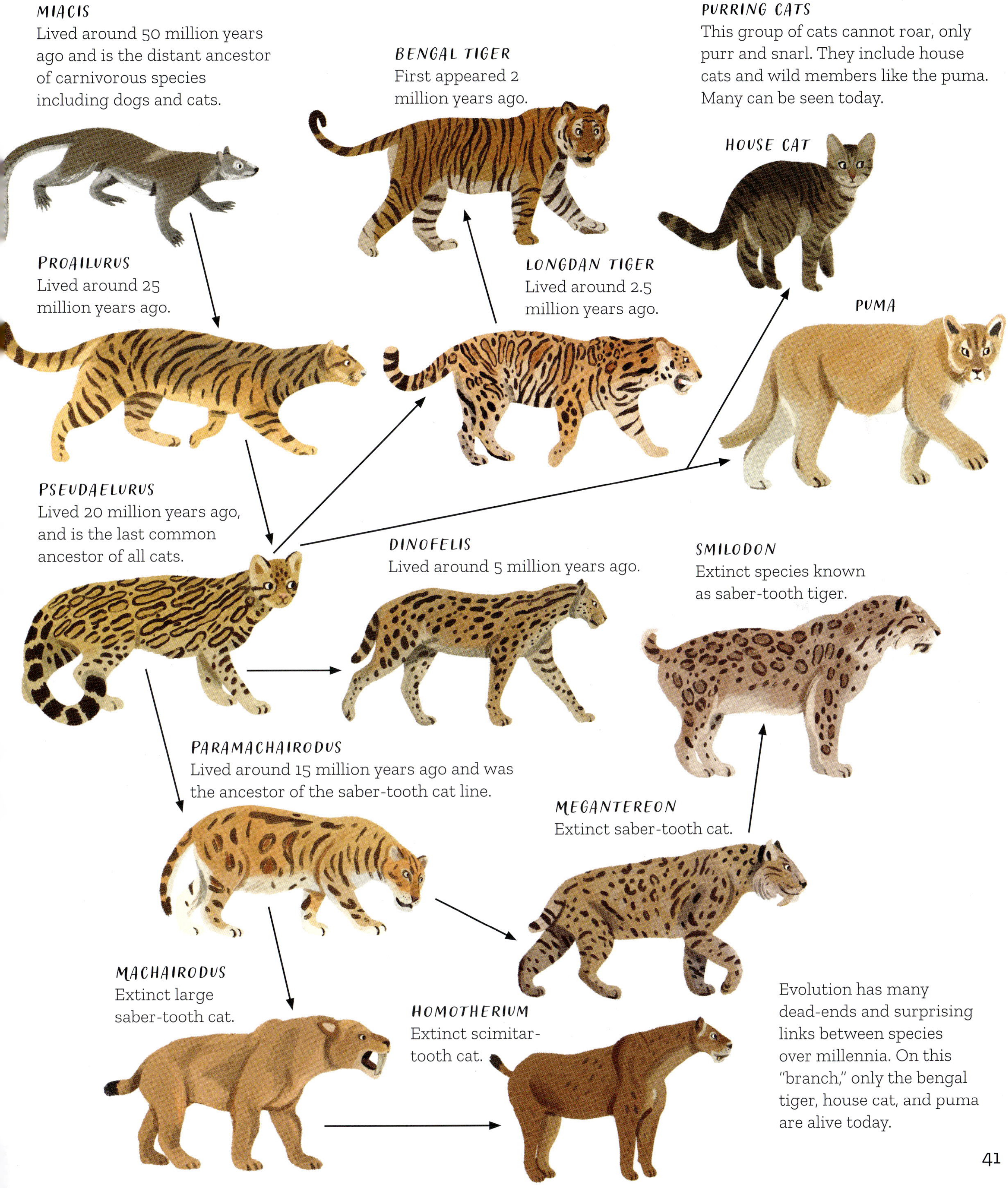

Evolution has many dead-ends and surprising links between species over millennia. On this "branch," only the bengal tiger, house cat, and puma are alive today.

THE WEB OF LIFE

Origin showed that species are dependent on each other for survival. Their web of relationships can be competitive or cooperative. Animals may fight to hold territory, and plants may struggle against each other in the search for light. They may feed on each other, or help each other out.

Savanna Stories

African grasslands contain many different species with their own survival needs, but they are all connected in the same ecosystem. For example, antelope are plant-eaters, so they eat the grass. Cheetahs are meat-eaters, so they hunt the antelope.

Everything is in balance. Remove one element and it threatens the whole ecosystem. If the cheetahs disappear, the antelope population will grow so quickly they risk running out of food. If the grass vanishes, the antelopes will die out, and therefore so will the cheetahs. Over millions of years, species in every habitat have evolved to become linked.

Companions

Some species have evolved a very close link to another species. Oxpeckers spend their lives clambering all over big animals, such as rhinos, eating the ticks and blood-sucking insects that cling to the mammal's skin. This provides oxpeckers with food, while the rhino's skin is cleared of parasites. Oxpeckers are also excellent lookouts, screaming alarm calls if a predator appears. The Swahili name for oxpecker is *Askari Wa Kifaru*—"The Rhino's Guard."

Hummingbirds and Red Angel's Trumpets

Flowers need to be pollinated to produce seeds. Pollinators—such as bugs, birds, and bats—are attracted by food in the form of nectar. But most pollen is wasted when it is carried to the wrong species of plants. Some flowers have evolved a shape that solves this problem. Inside the long red angel's trumpet flowers, nectar is well hidden. Only sword-billed hummingbirds have beaks long enough to reach this food. As the hummingbirds feed, pollen sticks to their beaks and is then carried to other flowers of the same species.

The hummingbird's strange beak makes it difficult to feed from other kinds of flowers, so they keep returning to red angel's trumpets, guaranteeing the plant's pollination. As a reward, the sword-billed hummingbirds are well fed.

SWORD-BILLED HUMMINGBIRD (ENSIFERA ENSIFERA) FEEDING FROM RED ANGEL'S TRUMPET (BRUGMANSIA SANGUINEA)

THE SLOW MARCH OF EVOLUTION

Darwin made it clear that evolution by natural selection was not a fast process. It involved small changes over vast time periods. Scientists now understand that life on Earth first appeared around 3.7 billion years ago. Fossils of tiny microscopic organisms called microbes have been found near hydrothermal vents—cracks in the ocean floor where seawater is heated by volcanic activity in the Earth's crust. It was around this time that the organism from which all life on Earth descended—the Last Universal Common Ancestor (LUCA)—lived.

Earth's History in 24 Hours

Looking at the entire life span of the Earth as a 24-hour clock helps us understand how slowly life has evolved.

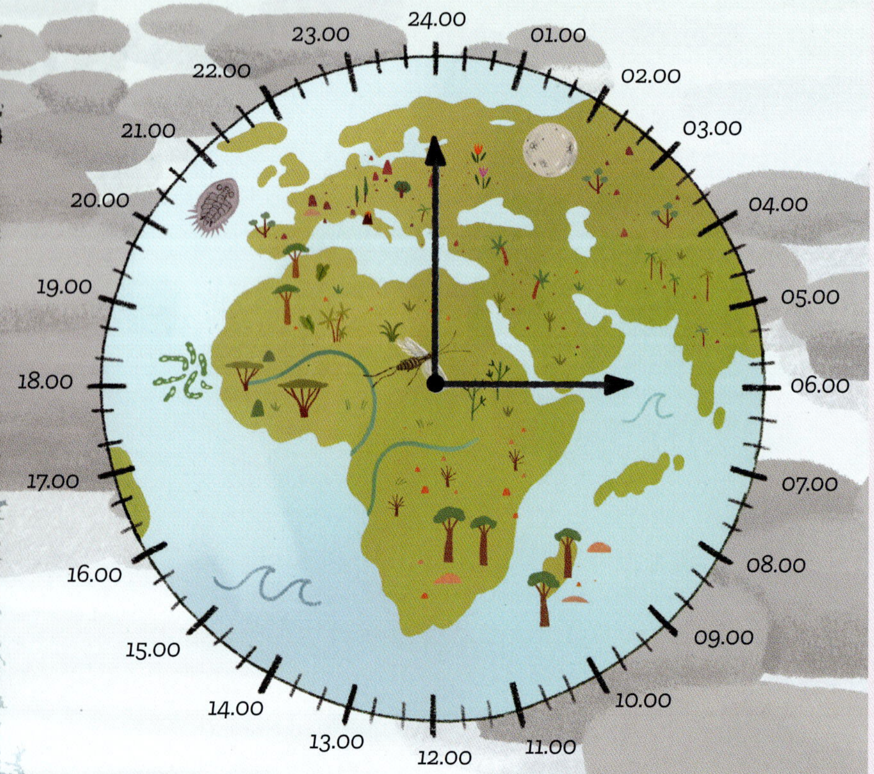

Looking at Earth's history in this way shows us just how recently humans evolved.

00.01 EARTH IS FORMED

00.01–03.00 EARTH IS VOLCANIC, SCALDING HOT WITH AN ATMOSPHERE FULL OF POISONOUS GASSES

03.15 FIRST ROCKS FORM

04.20 FIRST SINGLE-CELL LIFE APPEARS IN THE FORM OF MICROBES

05.30 FIRST FOSSILS ARE CREATED

08.00 LAST UNIVERSAL COMMON ANCESTOR APPEARS (LUCA)

09.00 BACTERIA BEGIN TO RELEASE OXYGEN

10.40 OXYGEN LEVELS START TO RISE

11.00 FIRST LAND BEGINS TO EMERGE ABOVE THE SEA

18.40 SIMPLE ALGAE STARTS TO GROW

21.20 FIRST FISH APPEAR

21.36 FIRST PLANTS GROW ON LAND

21.56 FIRST INSECTS EVOLVE

22.00 FORESTS/ JUNGLES DEVELOP

22.47 FIRST DINOSAURS EVOLVE

22.56 TINY MAMMALS APPEAR

23.15 BIRDS EVOLVE FROM DINOSAURS

23.40 MASS EXTINCTION EVENT—EARTH IS HIT BY AN ASTERIOD THAT WIPES OUT THE DINOSAURS

23.59 MODERN HUMANS APPEAR

Stromatolites

Shallow tropical seas are home to strange structures called stromatolites, one of the very first life forms that appeared on Earth. They are built by millions of marine microorganisms living together in one colony. To protect themselves, the organisms release a kind of glue that bonds together sand and tiny pieces of rock, to create what look like boulders.

Stromatolites are rare today, but thrived 3.5 billion years ago. Stromatolites played an important role in the evolution of life. Until they appeared, the Earth's atmosphere was toxic, and very little could survive. Some stromatolites used the Sun's energy to make food—this is photosynthesis, and it also produces oxygen. Over 2 billion years, the Earth's atmosphere changed, creating the first breathable air, and allowing countless other species to evolve.

RISE OF THE BIRDS

Darwin believed there were intermediate stages in evolution, where a species evolved from one form to another. We tend not to find these "transitional forms" living alongside species that have already adapted to their environment. This is because the latter will out-compete the "intermediate" for resources. Occasionally, the incomplete fossil record helps us to glimpse exciting moments in an evolutionary story.

From Dinosaur Beginnings

Dinosaurs ruled Earth for around 165 million years. As they grew bigger, competition increased for resources. Some theropods (a group of dinosaurs with hollow bones and three claws on each limb) evolved into smaller, more agile creatures. It was from these reptiles that birds would eventually emerge.

FOSSIL OF ARCHAEOPTERYX (ARCHAEOPTERYX LITHOGRAPHICA)

Transitional Fossil—Meet Archaeopteryx

In 1861, a fossil was discovered that supported Darwin's theory of transitional forms. It was a creature around 50 cm (20 in) long, with an estimated weight of 1 kg (2.2 lb). Archaeopteryx, as the fossil was named, is a transitional fossil because it had some characteristics of reptiles and some of birds. Archaeopteryx had the wings and feathers of birds, and the boney tail and teeth of reptiles. It lived around 147 million years ago.

Feathered Fossils—Later Discoveries

Found in 1999, the *Beipiaosaurus inexpectus* fossil has two kinds of feathers: downy ones for warmth, and longer ones for display. *Caudipteryx zoui*, discovered in 1998, has many of the characteristics that might be expected in a "missing link" between dinosaurs and birds, but it lived many millions of years after Archaeopteryx, the first known bird-like dinosaur.

BEIPIAOSAURUS INEXPECTUS

CAUDIPTERYX ZOUI

Dinosaur-Birds Today

Hoatzin (*Opisthocomus hoazin*) are probably the closest living species to early birdlike animals. Although they can fly, Hoatzin prefer to climb clumsily around the branches in South American rainforests. They are leaf-eaters, just like some of their reptile ancestors.

The Chicken or the Egg?

What did come first, the chicken or the egg? The answer is the egg, because birds inherited egg-laying from their dinosaur ancestors. Dinosaurs died out 65 million years ago, but the 11,000 bird species alive today are their descendants.

CONVERGENT EVOLUTION

As Darwin understood, evolution happens because of the advantages it produces. Unrelated species from completely different parts of the world can sometimes look similar and share the same habits. This is because they have evolved the most successful survival tools for similar environments. This is called convergent evolution.

Finding Your Niche

An environment or habitat and all the things living in it is called an ecosystem. A "niche" is a place within an ecosystem. Living things can evolve to fit a similar niche in different ecosystems. This is why some species with no genetic connection may look alike.

Birds of prey and owls were once thought to be part of the same family, because they look so alike. Both have forward-facing eyes, hooked beaks, and sharp talons. In fact, their similarities are all about their place as predators in the ecosystem. Eyes facing the same direction are essential to predators because they provide the best way of accurately judging the distance of prey; talons are the tools that catch prey; and sharp beaks are necessary to rip a tough meal apart.

Bottlenose Dolphin and Bull Shark

It can be difficult to tell bottlenose dolphins and bull sharks apart. Dolphins are mammals and sharks are fish, but because they share the same habitat and eat the same food, they have evolved bodies that are quite similar. Flat, powerful tails drive them through the water; fins on the side and back keep the animals stable; and a streamlined body helps them cut through the water with ease.

A VERY FISHY BULL SHARK (CARCHARHINUS LEUCAS)

THE BOTTLENOSE DOLPHIN (TURSIOPS TRUNCATUS)—VERY MUCH A MAMMAL

Australian Echidna and European Hedgehog

Echidnas are strange Australian mammals that lay eggs and can detect electricity through their sensitive noses. European hedgehogs are very different. They live on the other side of the world and give birth to live babies. It is not a coincidence that the two species look similar. Both eat insects and other invertebrates. They do not need to move quickly to find food, but this lack of speed makes them targets for predators. So echidnas and hedgehogs have independently evolved a barrier of sharp spines that keep many enemies away.

THE PRICKLY EUROPEAN HEDGEHOG (ERINACEUS EUROPAEUS)

AUSTRALIA'S SPINY SHORT-BEAKED ECHIDNA (TACHYGLOSSUS ACULEATUS)

HOW LAND ON EARTH MOVED

Darwin struggled to understand how a species could appear in different places around the Earth. Did they appear in various locations at the same time? He eventually concluded that they originated in one place and then migrated to different places from there. However, this idea of migration (moving to new environments) is only part of the story. Another reason is the movement of landmasses.

Continental Drift

We now know that when the first plants and animals appeared on Earth, the world's continents were arranged differently. Around 550 million years ago, most land was concentrated together in one of the supercontinents called Gondwana. Land sits on floating slabs of the Earth's crust called tectonic plates. The plates are constantly moving—just a few cm (in) a year. But that movement mounts up to vast distances when it happens over millions of years. We call this "continental drift." As the continents separated, they became divided by oceans. This meant that some species became isolated from their relatives.

Climate Shifts

In addition to continental drift, changes in climate have an impact on sea levels. This means that some land becomes isolated, only to reconnect as the climate shifts again. This process, over many millions of years, allows species to migrate.

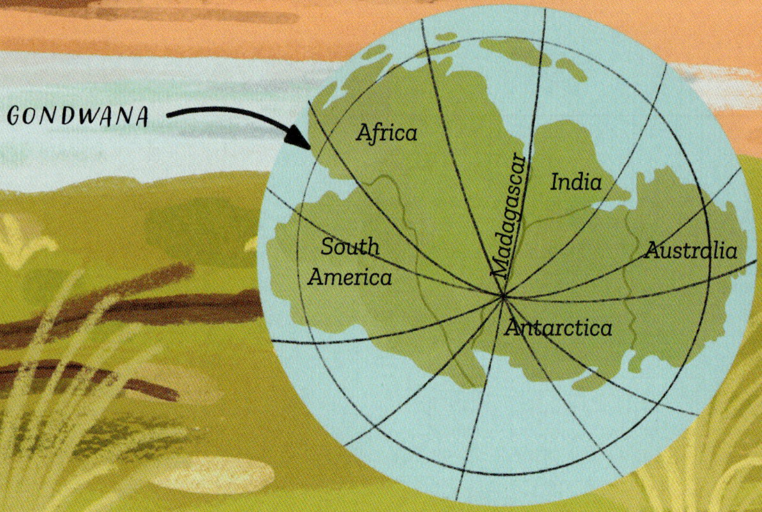

Antarctic Surprises

Land that was once in the tropics moved slowly to the polar regions. Some species evolved; others died out. Today, on average, the ice covering the Antarctic is 2 km (1.24 miles) thick, and the temperature can drop to -50°C (-58°F). But the rock beneath the ice tells a different story. There are fossils that show the continent was once a thriving rainforest, and home to a diverse range of animals.

Meet Cryolophosaurus

Cryolophosaurus ellioti was a 7 m (23 ft) long carnivorous dinosaur. A one-of-a-kind fossil of the creature was discovered under the Beardmore Glacier in Antarctica. As the continent drifted slowly toward the South Pole, the falling temperatures would have made dinosaur survival impossible.

SCIENCE TODAY
THE DISCOVERY OF THE GENE

Darwin understood that plants and animals passed on characteristics to their offspring, but it was nearly 100 years before scientists discovered how the process worked. In 1953, scientists made a discovery that helped unlock the secrets of the gene—the software that controls every feature of life, such as petal shape, height, and temperament.

DNA

In sexual reproduction, living things inherit genes from their two parents—half from the male, and half from the female. Genes are made up of DNA. Living things reproduce by copying DNA (deoxyribonucleic acid) and passing it on to their offspring. But DNA does not duplicate itself perfectly; the process contains tiny faults. It is these faults that create the variants that drive evolution. DNA molecules are long, twisted ladders in a structure known as a "double helix." Genes are units of DNA, and they determine the characteristics of living things. Every species has its own unique set of genes.

DNA is a chain of four chemicals. A gene is a unique sequence of these four chemicals: adenine, thymine, cytosine, and guanine, which are abbreviated as A, T, C, and G. Scientists have worked out the entire gene sequence of humans, and it contains 3.2 billion letters!

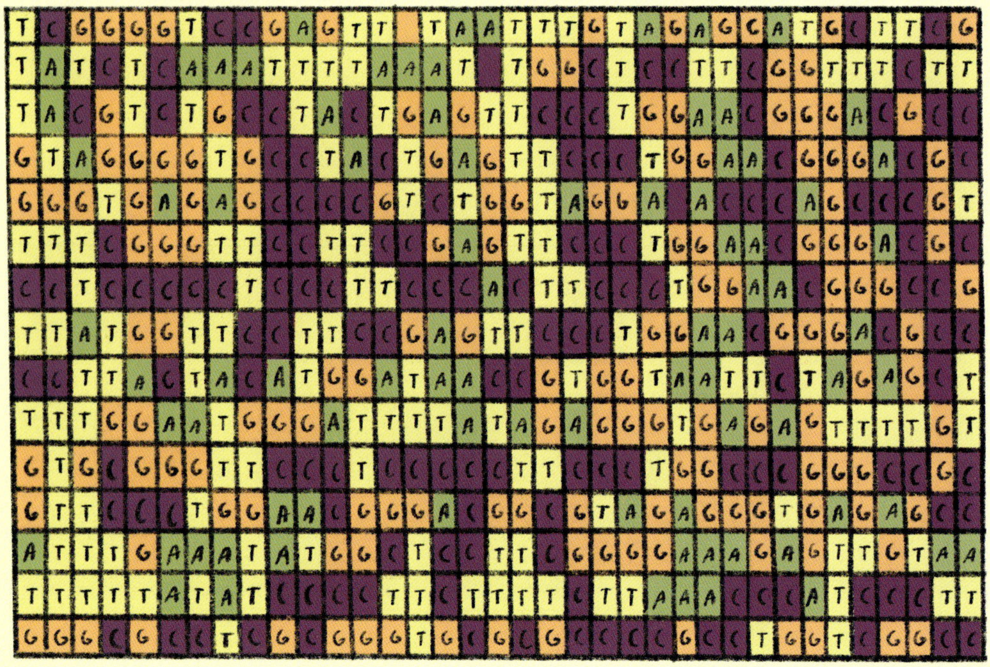

PART OF A GENOME SEQUENCE

PERCENTAGE OF GENES THAT HUMANS SHARE WITH OTHER SPECIES

Genetic Similarites

Many species contain identical genes, because such genes contain the basic instructions needed by all life—such as controllers for growth and reproduction. This means that humans share much of their DNA with other plants and animals.

Humans have around the same number of genes as a crab.

Family Connections

Until genes were discovered, plants and animals were put into families based on their physical appearance. Today, by looking at small differences in DNA, we can determine how closely related species are, and reveal how long ago they evolved. DNA has allowed scientists to uncover some unlikely family connections that were impossible to see in Darwin's time. For example, we now know that the closest relative to an elephant is the rock hyrax, an African animal the size of a rabbit.

The elephant and rock hyrax are more closely related than you might think.

THE ARRIVAL OF HUMANS

When Darwin published *The Descent of Man*, human evolution was an unknown science. But recent discoveries have revealed a family tree with many more members than we first imagined. All living humans belong to the species *Homo sapiens*, which first appeared around 200,000 years ago. We are the last in a long line of earlier human species that eventually became extinct. Humans belong to an order of mammals called primates, which includes apes. The ancestor of all primates was something like Plesiadapis, a small animal that looked rather like a squirrel.

Family Album

The great apes are our closest living relatives. We share about 99 percent of our DNA with the bonobos of Central Africa. But that 1 percent difference makes us quite distinct from them in appearance, intelligence, and habits.

LUCA

Darwin proposed the existence of an evolutionary starting point or organism from which all life descended. Scientists are still looking for a species that can be called the Last Universal Common Ancestor, known as "LUCA"—the organism from which all life on Earth evolved.

Last Common Ancestor

Apes and humans started to evolve separately around 6 million years ago. Both groups came from a species that scientists call the "last common ancestor" (LCA). Our ancestors were about the size of an eight-year-old human, with teeth that indicate they ate a wide variety of foods. Fossil evidence from skeletons suggests that they were well suited to life in the trees.

FACIAL RECONSTRUCTION OF THE LAST COMMON ANCESTOR (LCA) OF HUMANS AND APES

Human Journey

At least eight human species have evolved and disappeared. Neanderthals were one of the most recent, and they died out about 40,000 years ago. But they lived alongside modern humans for thousands of years. During this time, Neanderthals and modern humans interbred. There are millions of people alive today with Neanderthal DNA. It only amounts to about 2 percent of their genes, but forms part of the complicated mixture of traits that makes humans so successful.

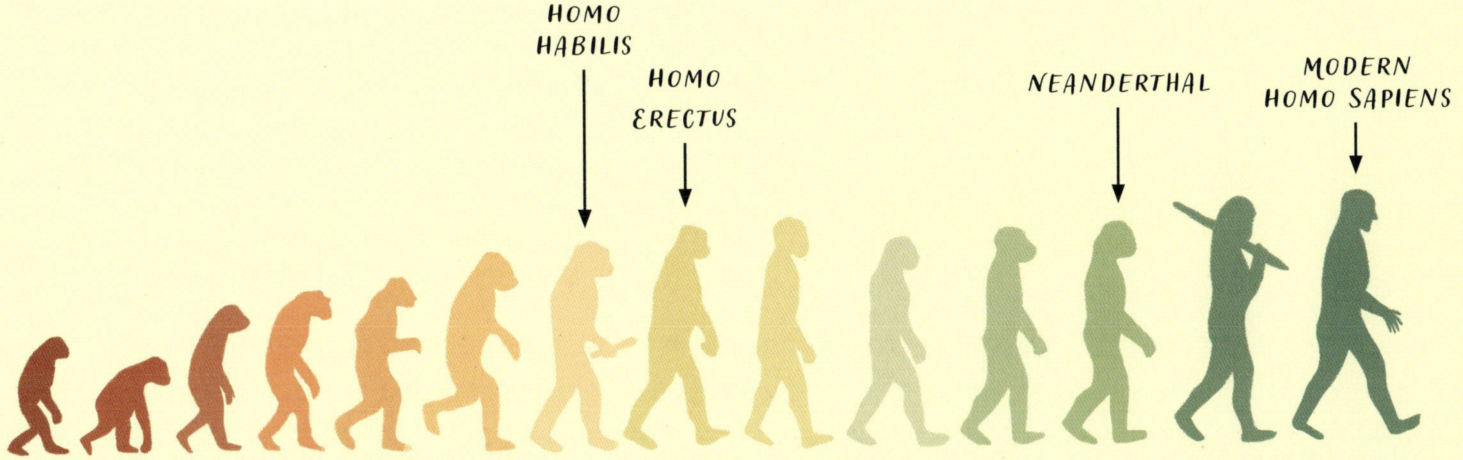

This famous picture shows the evolution of humans, but it gets a lot wrong. Humans did not evolve from chimpanzees as this seems to show. Instead, chimps and humans both evolved from the same long-gone early primate ancestor.

SOME THINGS DARWIN GOT WRONG ...

Advances in technology and the growth of scientific knowledge have led to new discoveries about the Earth and life on the planet. Some of this new information challenges what Darwin thought in the 1800s.

Age of the Earth

Darwin estimated that the Earth was around 100 million years old. But he admitted that this was little more than an educated guess. We now know that the Earth was formed 4.5 billion years ago.

Pangenesis

Darwin believed that animals that developed special characteristics during their lifetime would pass them on to their young. For example, he thought that if a bodybuilder developed powerful muscles, then their babies would have them too. Darwin called this idea "pangenesis," but it turned out to be wrong. Although bodybuilders had big muscles, their DNA did not change—and it was this that was passed on to their babies.

Blended Inheritance

In the 19th century, Darwin and other scientists developed a theory called "blended inheritance." They thought that a young animal would be an exact mixture of its mother and father. So if a black cat mated with a white cat, they would always produce black and white kittens. But scientists realized that the theory was wrong, because a black cat paired with a white cat can produce six kittens each with different variations of fur, including ginger and tabby. This is natural variation.

Extinction Events

Darwin believed that because evolution was a slow process, extinction must be equally slow. He was right in many cases, but he could not have known about single catastrophic events, such as the asteriod that hit the Earth 65 million years ago and wiped out most of the dinosaurs. During this mass extinction, around 76 percent of all species were wiped out. With fewer animals and, for a time, less competition, the pace and variety of evolution increased for a period.

GENE EDITING AND THE FUTURE OF EVOLUTION

Unthinkable in Darwin's lifetime, modern technology allows us to make small changes in DNA to produce characteristics that we want in crop plants and farm animals. Genes responsible for size, shade, or speed of growth can be taken out and replaced with genes from the same species that has the feature we need. This is gene editing, and it is much more efficient than traditional selective breeding techniques used by farmers.

Pest Control

Insect pests are one of the biggest problems faced by crop farmers. They can have a devastating impact on cereal harvests. Genetic modification can be used to limit this threat by making plants unattractive to insects. The genes of a cereal corn crop called Bt Maize have been changed so that the plants produce a natural poison that caterpillars will not eat. Farmers can now produce much greater harvests, as the young plants are no longer eaten by caterpillars.

Allergy Defense

Around 3 percent of young children are allergic to cow's milk, and this can create problems with growth and development. Scientists have slightly altered the genes of some cows so that their milk does not contain the chemical that triggers allergies. Genetically edited cows now produce milk that is much safer for children with allergies to drink.

Designer Eyes?

Gene editing has to be used with caution. For example, suppose would-be parents wanted to choose the eye or hair type of their child? While scientists have discovered that eye coloration is controlled by the gene OCA2, most scientists feel that editing should not be used to interfere with people's appearance. Today, gene editing is used only to improve food supply or combat health problems.

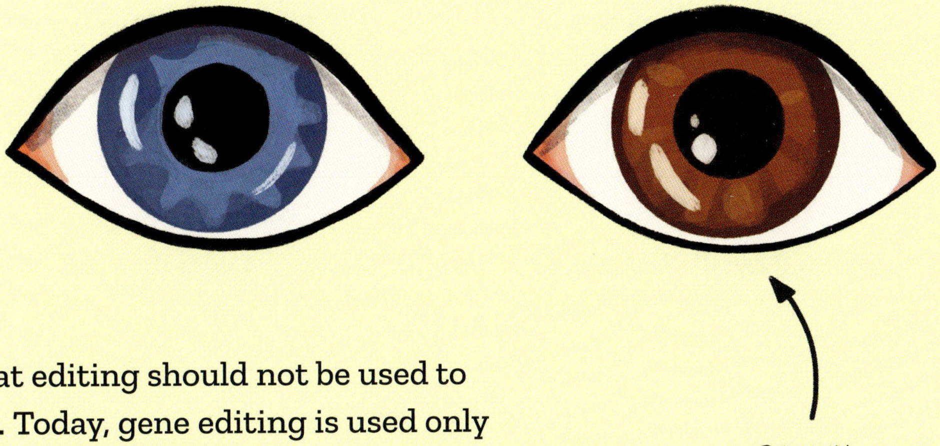

BROWN OR BLUE?

The Future of Gene Editing

The discovery of new, more efficient gene editing techniques mean scientists will be able to change the DNA of many more species. One day, it might be possible to combat conditions such as cancer. But like all new science, gene editing requires more research before it is fully understood.

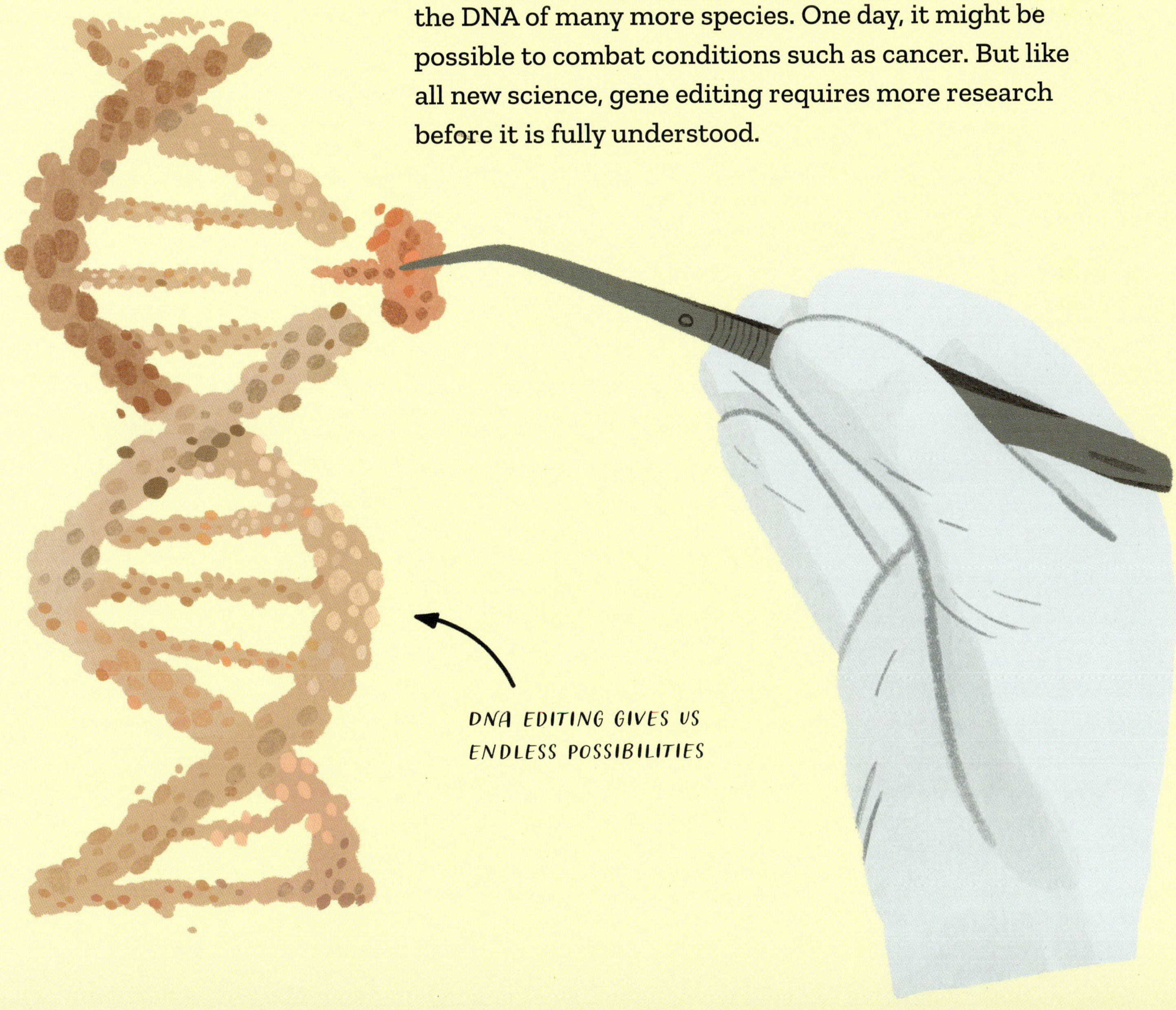

DNA EDITING GIVES US ENDLESS POSSIBILITIES

EVOLUTION IN ACTION

Evolution is usually a slow process, because habitats and climate do not change overnight. But human activity has accelerated change. Forests can disappear as cities expand, and new roads are built where there were once meadows. So in order to survive, animals must adapt to a completely new environment.

Urbanization

As cities grow, more plants and animals move into them. This is a modern form of natural selection. Species that can change their diet and habits to fit the new habitat stand a better chance of survival than those that cannot. But it is too soon to know if these animals will change physically as they make the shift from countryside to city.

RED FOX (VULPES VULPES)
Rural foxes hunt rabbits and mice in woodlands, but urban foxes eat rats and food discarded by humans.

CITY PIGEON (COLUMBA LIVIA DOMESTICA)
Millions of pigeons have settled into urban life, feeding on scraps of human food.

KESTREL (FALCO TINNUNCULUS)
Heat produced by cars, people, and buildings makes cities much warmer than the surrounding countryside. To a kestrel, a windowsill is much the same as a cliff face—only less cold.

GARDEN BIRDS
Small birds face starvation in winter as their natural food disappears. Some now feed on bird tables stocked all year round by humans.

PEREGRINE (FALCO PEREGRINUS)
Peregrines have moved into cities because there are many more pigeons to eat.

COYOTE (CANIS LATRANS)
The rats and mice that follow humans into the city attract coyotes.

FALLOW DEER (DAMA DAMA)
City deer now feed in parks and gardens.

Bear Facts

Grizzly bears are creatures of the northern forests, but because of climate change, the Arctic is growing warmer, and grizzlies are moving further north into icy polar bear territory. The two species are related, but would normally never meet. Climate change is pushing the two together, and they have produced offspring.

Today, there are occasional sightings of a completely new bear, a cross between a polar bear and a grizzly. Science has not yet given them a name, but local people call them grolar bear, pizzly bear, or the grizzlar.

GLOSSARY

ADAPTATION—Changing to better fit an environment or condition.

AMBER—Hardened resin produced by trees.

ANCESTOR—An earlier form of animal or plant from which later species have evolved.

BACTERIA—A huge group of organisms that have bodies made from just one cell.

CETACEAN—A family of mammals that includes all whales and dolphins.

CO-EVOLUTION—The evolution of two or more species who rely on or benefit from each other.

CONVERGENT EVOLUTION—The evolution of two or more unrelated species to look and behave in similar ways.

DESCENDANTS—Living things that have evolved from the same ancestors.

DNA (DEOXYRIBONUCLEIC ACID)—Long strands of chemicals inside all living cells that carry genetic information.

ECOSYSTEM—A complex community of living things and the habitat in which they live.

EMBRYO—An unborn animal that is still inside an egg or its mother.

EVOLUTION—Gradual changes that take place in plants and animals over long periods of time.

FOSSIL—Ancient remains or traces of plants or animals preserved inside rock.

GENES— Small sections of DNA that determine what traits are passed down from parent to child.

GENOME—The complete set of genes that exist in a living thing or species.

GEOLOGY—The science that explores the history of the Earth through its rocks.

GONDWANA—An ancient supercontinent that contained most of the Earth's land before it broke up around 180 million years ago.

HABITAT—The environment in which an animal or plant normally lives.

MICROBES—Tiny living creatures that can only be seen through a microscope.

NATURALIST—A person who studies living things and their environments.

NATURAL SELECTION—The process by which the living things best adapted to their environment survive and reproduce, while the less well adapted die out.

NECTAR—A sweet liquid produced by flowers to attract pollinators.

POLLEN—Powder produced by flowers. It contains male cells that need to be added to female cells so that the plant can produce seeds.

POLLINATION—Moving pollen from one plant to another to allow flowering plants to reproduce.

PREDATOR—An animal that hunts and eats other animals.

PRIMATES—A group of mammals that includes lemurs, monkeys, apes, and humans.

REPRODUCTION—The process by which living things replicate themselves.

SELECTIVE BREEDING—The process by which humans choose which living things to breed together in order to produce desired characteristics in their offspring. Also known as "artificial breeding" or "domestic selection."

SEXUAL SELECTION—The kind of natural selection in which mates are selected for certain traits or characteristics—like long horns or a loud call—even though these traits do not aid in survival and, in fact, may hinder it.

TRANSTITIONAL FORMS—Species in the process of changing from one form to another.

VARIATION— Differences between individuals of the same species.